HERE COME
THE
ROBOTS

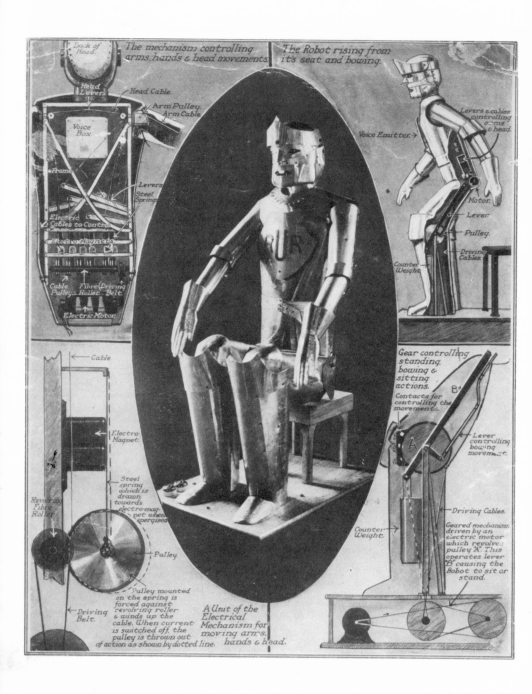

The mechanism controlling arms, hands & head movements.

The Robot rising from it's seat and bowing.

Back of Head.

Head Lever.

Head Cable.

Arm Pulley.
Arm Cable.

Voice Box.

Voice Emitter.→

Frame.

Levers & cables controlling arms & head.

Levers.
Steel Spring.

Motor.

Lever.

Electric Cables to Control.

Pulley.

Electro Magnets.

Driving Cables.

Cable Pulleys.
Fibre (Driving) Roller. Belt.

Counter Weight.

Electric Motor.

Gear controlling standing, bowing & sitting actions.

Cable.→

B.

Contacts for controlling the movements.

Electro-Magnet.→

A.

Lever controlling bowing movement.

Revolving Fibre Roller.

Steel spring which is drawn towards electro-magnet when energised.

Driving Cables.

Pulley.

Counter Weight.

Geared mechanism driven by an electric motor which revolves pulley "A". This operates lever "B" causing the Robot to sit or stand.

Driving Belt.

Pulley mounted on the spring is forced against revolving roller & winds up the cable. When current is switched off, the pulley is thrown out of action as shown by dotted line.

A Unit of the Electrical Mechanism for moving arms, hands & head.

HERE COME THE ROBOTS

by

JOYCE MILTON

Illustrated with photographs, prints,

and cartoons by Peter Stern

HASTINGS HOUSE · PUBLISHERS

New York

Library of Congress Cataloging in Publication Data

Milton, Joyce.   Here come the robots.

Bibliography: p.
Includes index.
Summary: Discusses the history of robots, real robots that have existed, and some fictional ones.
1. Automata—Juvenile literature.   2. Robots, Industrial—Juvenile literature.   [1. Robots.   2. Automata]
I. Title.
TJ211.M54   629.8′92   81-2476
ISBN 0-8038-6363-2   AACR2

Published simultaneously in Canada by
Saunders of Toronto, Ltd., Don Mills, Ontario

Printed in the United States of America

CONTENTS

Acknowledgments   7

Real Robots   11
The Age of Automatons   15
Here Come the Robots   25
Building a Better Mouse   31
Robots Go to Work   37
Blue Collar Robots   41
Robots, Robots Everywhere   47
A Robot in the House   55
Cyborgs: Part Man—Part Machine   65
Robots in Outer Space   73
Talking Robots   83
Robot Hoaxes   87
Robots: Good and Evil   89

Robots of Tomorrow   95
Glossary: What Is a Robot?   101
Robot Records   103

Picture Credits   111
Bibliography   113
Index   115

Acknowledgments

Grateful acknowledgment is made to the following individuals and organizations for their assistance:
Lori D. Mei, of the Robot Institute of America;
IEEE Computer Society, sponsors of the Amazing Micro-Mouse contest;
Vernon E. Estes, Manager, Process Automation & Control Systems, General Electric Corporation;
Peggy A. Wallace, Ph.D., University of Southern California School of Medicine, for information about SIM ONE;
Dr. Michael J. Freeman, for information about LEACHIM;
Ellen D. Mohr of Unimation Robotics, Unimation, Inc.;
Cincinnati Milacron, Inc.;
Westinghouse Electric Company;
Hughes Aircraft Company;
Quasar Industries, Inc.;
National Aeronautics and Space Administration.

HERE COME
THE
ROBOTS

R2-D2 and C3PO of Star Wars fame.

REAL ROBOTS

The robot is a science fiction fantasy come true.

The first robots were imaginary beings. They existed only in the minds of writers and artists. Later, imaginary robots starred in scores of movies and TV shows. Some of these robots were friendly and lovable, like R2-D2 and C3PO of *Star Wars* fame. Most were pure trouble.

Everyone knows about these imaginary robots. This book will tell you about some robots you may not know about—real robots.

Real robots are every bit as interesting and strange as imaginary ones. Sometimes they are even stranger.

Just for fun, try to guess which of the robots named on this page are real and which are imaginary.

The answers to this "robot quiz" are on the next page. But here's a hint to get you started: four of the robots here are real; three are not.

1. ROBBIE is a robot babysitter. He can play hide-and-seek and carry children piggyback. But he cannot speak.

2. MOXON'S ROBOT is a robot chess player in the form of a man.

3. SULLA is a robot typist. She can type in four languages.

4. THE SPACE HORSE is a robot horse that astronauts can ride as they explore the surfaces of distant planets.

5. ELEKTRO is a seven-foot-tall talking robot. He travels with his robot dog, SPARKO.

6. AROK is a robot servant. He can run a vacuum cleaner, take out the garbage, answer the door, and even walk the dog.

7. RMIU—short for Robot Mobile Investigation Unit—is a robot in the service of the Royal Canadian Mounted Police. He always gets his man.

A robot babysitter.

Did you guess that the first three robots were the imaginary ones?

Moxon's robot appeared in a story written by Ambrose Bierce in 1913. This imaginary robot was good at chess but a sore loser. When he lost a game, he went on a rampage and killed Moxon, the man who had invented him.

Sulla, the robot typist, was a character in a play called *Rossum's Universal Robots,* or *R.U.R.* The author of this play, Karel Čapek, was the first person to use the word *robot.*

Machines that play chess or type have been invented in the years since these imaginary characters first appeared. Unfortunately, no one has yet invented a robot like Robbie—he would probably be a lot more fun than a real babysitter. Robbie first appeared in a story by science fiction writer Isaac Asimov. Later, another Robbie the robot starred in several movies, including one called *Forbidden Planet.*

The last four robots mentioned in the quiz are the real robots. You will learn more about them later on.

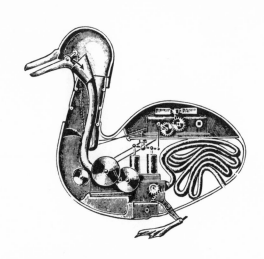

THE AGE OF AUTOMATONS

The idea of building a "mechanical man" is very, very old. Many hundreds of years ago, before machines were used to do much everyday work, wealthy people collected mechanical toys to amaze and amuse their friends.

Some Japanese homes had dolls that could serve tea to guests. The dolls held trays in front of them. When a full cup of tea was placed on its tray, the doll would bow and begin to walk forward. When the guest took the cup of tea, the doll stopped walking.

Chinese emperors owned more complicated mechanical toys such as dancing girls and musicians that actually played tunes. One emperor of

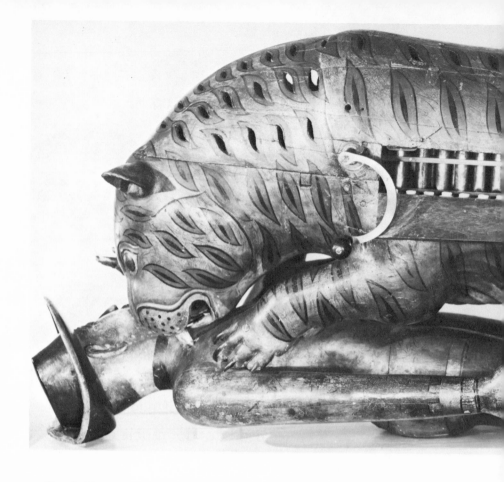

Tipu's Tiger, a six-foot-long mechanical toy that belonged to the sultan of Mysore in India. When the toy is set in motion, the tiger growls fiercely while his victim, a British soldier, waves his arms and screams.

Byzantium is said to have owned a mechanical lion that roared. If the emperors' guests were frightened by these toys, so much the better. The rumor would spread that these rulers had magic powers!

One of the most unusual collections of mechanical toys belonged to a noble family in France six hundred years ago. This family had a room filled with wooden figures that would spray unsuspecting guests with water, flour, and feathers. It seems that the guests thought this was very funny.

Another story about a wonderful mechanical toy comes from fifteenth century Spain. It is said that a wealthy nobleman, Don Alvaro de Luna, ordered a mechanical tombstone. When Don Al-

An eighteenth century tea doll from Japan, made with cogs, springs, and whales' whiskers.

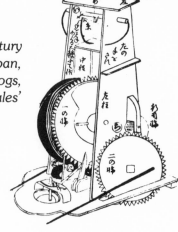

A toy knife-grinder cart made in France in the 1700s.

A group of water-powered statues built in 1589. When struck with the club, the dragon spits water in the man's face.

During the Middle Ages, clockwork "mechanical men" like this one were used to strike the bells of many town clocks.

varo and his wife died, they were buried inside the main church of Toledo, Spain. The mechanical figures of the Don and his lady lay on top of the tomb, and every time the congregation knelt to pray, the figures would rise to their knees and pray, too!

We can't be sure that this story is true because Don Alvaro's tombstone does not exist today. It is said that Queen Isabella had it smashed. Not surprisingly, she thought that the moving figures on the tombstone would make it hard for the churchgoers to pay attention to the service.

Some stories about old mechanical toys, like the one about Don Alvaro's tombstone, may have been made up. But we do know how a number of these toys worked. Some were powered by water or by steam—centuries before the invention of the first steam engine. Most had the kind of gears normally used in clocks.

Of course, no one called these toys *robots*. The word didn't even exist. They were called *automatons*, which means something that moves by its own power. Mechanical toys that looked like men and women were also called *androids*—a word that means "manlike."

By the eighteenth century, it was possible to build very realistic looking androids. The most amazing of all were created by the Jaquet-Droz family of Switzerland. One of their inventions was in the form of a little boy seated at a desk. It could

The Writer, a famous Jaquet-Droz android, could write messages up to forty characters long.

write any message up to forty letters long. This was done by adjusting gears inside the android's chest. Of course, the gears had to be reset again every time the operator wanted the boy to write a different message.

The Jaquet-Droz androids were so lifelike that some people were frightened by them. One member of the family was accused of witchcraft. And Mary Shelley, who saw the androids in 1816, probably had them in mind when she wrote the famous horror story *Frankenstein* a year later.

Other people were fooled into thinking that the androids really were almost human. In 1769, a con man named Baron von Kempelen displayed an automaton in the shape of a Turkish man seated at a desk. He claimed that his "mechanical Turk" could play chess—not just a little bit, but well enough to beat even good chess players.

Many famous people were taken in by this hoax. Even the French Emperor Napoleon I played chess with the Turk. And he lost.

Years later, the American short story writer Edgar Allan Poe had a chance to match his wits with the mechanical chess player. But unlike Napoleon, he was not fooled. Poe reasoned that the

Baron von Kempelen's Turkish chess player.

desk where the Turk sat had a secret compartment. A dwarf or a very small man would sit inside it and use levers to move the Turk's hand.

Poe never had a chance to test his theory, but it was later discovered that a human chess champion had been hidden inside the Turk.

In Poe's day, there was no such thing as a machine that could play chess. Automatons had moving parts, but they did not have brains. Many people thought machines never would be able to think. But they were wrong.

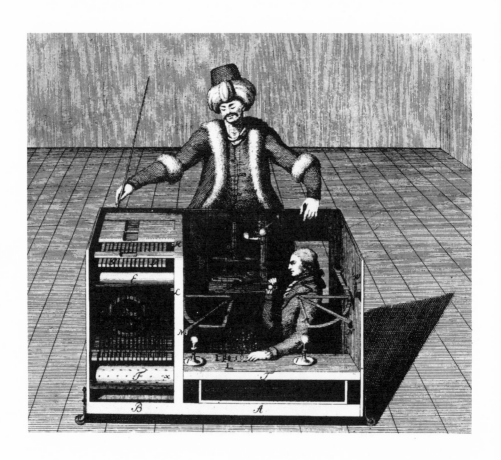

HERE COME THE ROBOTS

In 1921, Karel Čapek's play *Rossum's Universal Robots* was produced for the first time. It told the story of a greedy factory owner who creates a race of artificial men and women to replace his human workers. In the end, the artificial workers rebel against their human masters and take over the world.

Čapek called the workers in his play *robots*, a name he borrowed from a word in the Czech language which means "worker." This new name caught on, and soon it became more popular than the old word, *automaton*. In 1926, director Fritz

Lang made an evil robot named Maria the villain-ess in his movie *Metropolis,* and the robot was on its way to becoming a familiar character in films, stories, and comic books.

Robots came into the world at a time when new inventions—such as the automobile, the ra-dio and electric appliances—were making big changes in people's everyday lives. The robot came to stand for everything that was fun and a little bit frightening about the new machines that everyone had to cope with.

By the 1930's robots had become a fad. The public was no longer satisfied with the imaginary robots that they saw in the movies or read about in books and magazines. They wanted to see the real thing. For a time, no fair or civic celebration was complete without a robot.

One of the robot stars of this era was Alpha, a female robot shown at the London Radio Ex-position of 1932. Alpha was a very impressive-looking robot indeed, with shiny, chrome-plated skin and huge eyes and ears. She would bow to the audience, tell time, sing, and even smoke ci-gars! Alpha also amazed crowds at the exhibition by reading aloud from the morning newspapers.

The evil robot Maria with director Fritz Lang during the filming of the movie Metropolis.

Alpha, also known as "The Roboter," was the star of the London Radio Exposition of 1932.

Actually, Alpha could not read—this part of her performance was prerecorded.

The New York World's Fair of 1939 introduced two new robot performers—Elektro and his robot dog, Sparko. Elektro could walk, count on

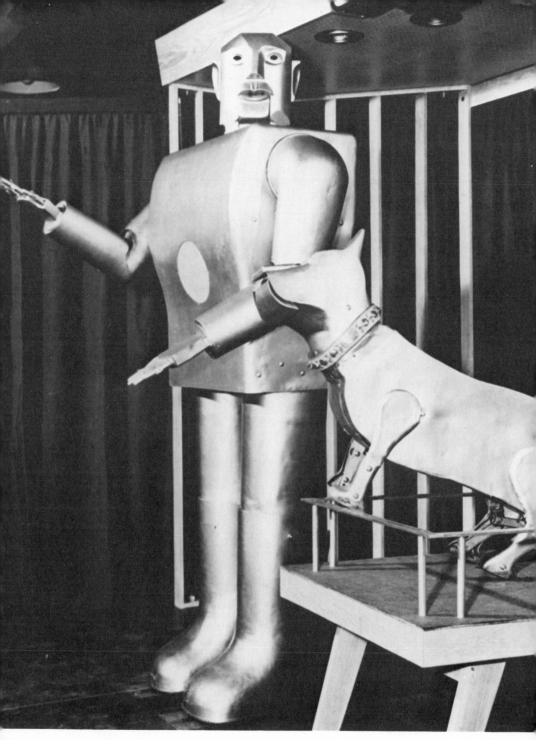

Elektro and his robot dog Sparko.

his fingers, tell the difference between the colors red and green, and give commands to Sparko. Sparko could bark and wag his tail. Elektro's greatest talent was his ability to obey spoken commands. To the audiences who gathered to watch Elektro perform, it seemed that he could understand English. But in reality, Elektro did not understand a word that was said to him. It was the timing and the number of syllables in the commands that gave him his cues.

In the same year, the first company to build robots for sale was formed. Mechanical Men, Inc. specialized in designing robots for store windows and displays. One of its most popular models was a robot made out of oil cans which was used to welcome customers at gas stations.

By this time, however, people had begun to realize the performing robots were just a new kind of mechanical toy. Alpha and Elektro were fun to see, but they could not compare to the imaginary robots of film and fiction. Like all fads, the robot craze died away as quickly as it had begun.

BUILDING A BETTER MOUSE

Just as the public became bored with robots, the scientific world got really interested in them. For the scientists, how a robot looked wasn't very important. The real challenge was to build machines that could actually function like human beings.

According to the scientists' definition, there was an important difference between a robot and other kinds of machines. First of all, a true robot would have to have some way of getting information about the outside world—just as a person does with his eyes, ears, nose, and sense of touch.

Then the robot would have to be able to use this information to change its behavior—in short, it would have to have a brain.

Building a robot that would be as smart as a human being was out of the question. In fact, some experts predicted that such a mechanical brain would be so large that it would fill London's huge cathedral Westminster Abbey! This was a discouraging thought, but it did not stop some scientists from trying to figure out how to build electronic brains. If the human brain was too complicated, they would just have to look for something simpler to copy.

One of these scientists was a psychologist named William Grey Walter who was interested in studying the brains of small animals. Dr. Walter wanted to see whether he could build a machine that could learn just the way an animal does. The result was the world's first robot turtles—Elmer and Elsie.

Elmer and Elsie turned out to be very successful robots. They could move around the floor without bumping into the furniture. When an obstacle was near, they sensed its presence and changed course. They even "knew" when their

The Moonlight Special, a robot mouse with a five inch square electronic brain.

batteries needed recharging. When this happened, they would head back to their "hutch" under their own power, just like hungry pets lining up for chow.

In 1952, only four years after Elmer and Elsie were constructed, computer pioneer Claude Shannon built another robot animal—a mouse. Just like a live laboratory rat, this robot mouse could learn to find its way through a maze. The first time, the robot would find its way by trial and error. Later, it could "remember" the correct path.

Micromouse Charlotte looking a bit frazzled after her big day.

Although it has been many years since Claude Shannon's invention, building a robot as smart as a mouse is still a big challenge. In 1977, the computer magazine *spectrum* announced its first Amazing Micro-Mouse contest, with a $1,000 grand prize for the robot mouse that could run a maze the fastest. More than 6,000 people, mostly engineers and students, entered the contest. But designing a smart mouse turned out to be more difficult than many of the contestants had expected.

On the day of the race only fifteen micro-mice showed up. Of these fifteen, nine robot mice—including Mikey, Mazey, and Charlotte—failed to get through the maze even once. Another mouse, named Catty-Wampus, had a very complex brain, but unfortunately, its designers couldn't control the mouse's speed. Their robot zoomed out of the starting gate so fast that it kept crashing into the walls of the maze and getting stuck.

In spite of everything, a few of the robot mice did very well indeed. The winner of the contest, Midnight Flash, ran the maze in thirty seconds, ten seconds faster than its nearest rival, Harvey Wallbanger. This was a record that any rodent would envy.

At first, it may seem strange that grown-up engineers would devote hundreds of hours to building robot mice. But projects such as the Amazing Micro-Mouse contest have a serious purpose.

Ever since Claude Shannon's time, mathematicians and engineers have been trying to think of new ways to use computers to do more than just solve mathematical problems or store information. One possibility was to give an electronic brain a mechanical body. This idea led to the creation of the first robots that were practical enough, and small enough, to earn their own way in the world.

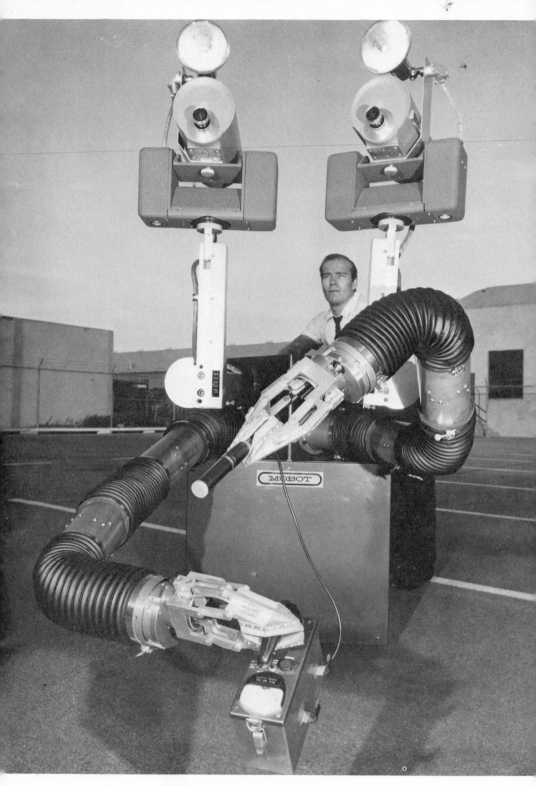

Using a geiger counter to test for radioactivity was one of the jobs of the early Mobot industrial robots.

ROBOTS GO TO WORK

The first working robots were invented to do jobs that were too dangerous for human beings.

The Mobot—short for Mobile Robot—was developed in the late 1950's to work in the radioactive areas of nuclear power plants. It has long, flexible arms with padded hands that can do many tricky jobs, such as pouring radioactive liquids from one test tube to another. The Mobot's "eyes" are two television cameras attached to movable stalks, just like the eyes of some insects.

When a human worker switches from one job to another, he or she uses different kinds of tools.

With a robot, it is actually possible to add "arms," "legs," and other parts that will make the job easier. Some Mobots are mounted on tank treads. Others have a crane attachment for moving heavy objects. There is no reason why a robot has to look just like a person, as long as it does the work.

There are even underwater versions of the Mobot. One of these is called UNUMO—or Universal Underwater Mobot. It looks like an enor-

This version of an underwater robot carries a human passenger.

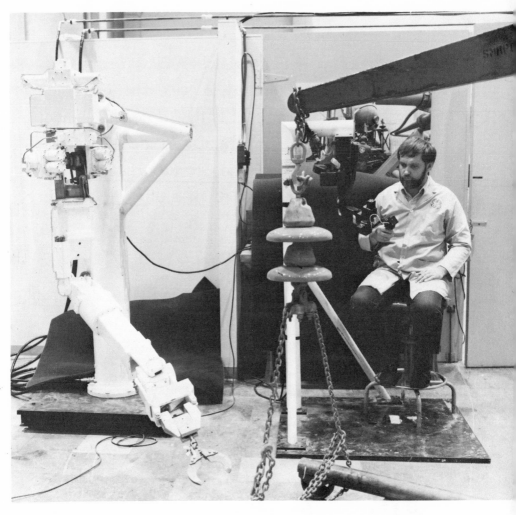

Another underwater robot, this one operated by remote control.

mous person in a deep-sea diving suit. Underwater robots have been used to explore the ocean floor, salvage sunken ships and repair off-shore oil rigs.

All of these robots work by remote control. They take orders from a human operator who sits at a control panel and watches television pictures taken by the robot's camera eyes. The interesting thing about such robots is that it doesn't matter whether the human operator is in the same room or many miles away. The operator may even be safe on earth, while the robot is at work in outer space.

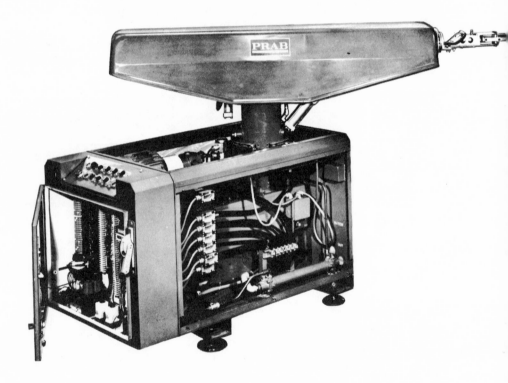

An industrial robot in use for over ten years.

BLUE COLLAR ROBOTS

WANTED: A factory worker who can do paint spraying, welding, heavy lifting, and many other jobs. Must be willing to do the most unpleasant work in our factory. Work 24 hours a day—no time off. POSITIVELY NO SALARY OR BENEFITS.

No human being would even answer this ad. But it sounds like a perfect opportunity for a robot.

Robot workers—also called "blue collar robots"—are becoming a familiar sight in many factories. A few years ago such robots were rare. In 1976, there were only 6,000 of them in the whole

A "blue collar robot" at work on an automobile assembly line.

world. Now there are eleven companies in the United States alone that do nothing but manufacture blue collar robots. And it has been predicted that by the end of the 1980's one out of every five hundred factory jobs will be done by a robot. In some kinds of factories, such as those that make automobiles, the proportion of robots to human workers will be much greater.

The typical blue collar robot is very ugly. It has a computer-controlled brain and one long arm. It has no face at all. But compared to such good-looking robots as Alpha and Elektro, the blue collar robot is quite smart. It doesn't need a boss standing over it. If a foreman wants to give the robot new instructions, he or she just reprograms the robot's brain, using a hand-held computer terminal that looks like a cross between a walkie-talkie and a push-button telephone.

The newer blue collar robots even have vision. Not only can they hold a television camera and take pictures—they interpret those pictures

A diagram of a modern industrial robot.

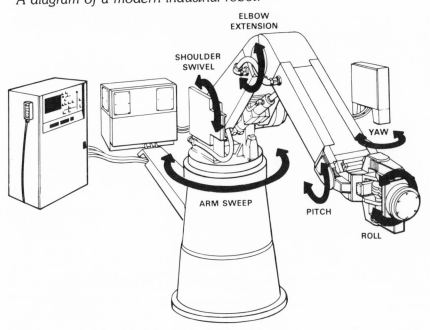

ELBOW
EXTENSION

SHOULDER
SWIVEL

YAW

ARM SWEEP

PITCH

ROLL

without human help. These "seeing" robots can inspect the work done by other robots.

Of course, the ultimate development would be an entire factory staffed entirely by robots. One such factory has already been built in Japan. It does have a single human employee, however, just to keep an eye on things. The Japanese hope to sell robot-run factories to other countries around the world.

Employers are usually happy to make the change from human workers to artificial ones. They like their mechanical employees because they never get bored, never take time off, and seldom make mistakes.

But when a robot does make a mistake, it is likely to be a big one. In one factory, a robot paint sprayer went berserk and started painting people instead of auto parts. Another robot was being shown off to a group of buyers when it suddenly began smashing itself to bits, right in the middle of the proud designer's sales talk. A human worker can take a little bit of mess and confusion in stride. But when a robot gets "confused," it goes to pieces—sometimes literally.

Of course, another reason why employers

In one factory, a robot paint sprayer went berserk and started painting people instead of auto parts.

like robots is that machines don't get paid. This is wonderful for the employer, but not so good for human workers who have to worry about losing their jobs to robots.

Ideally, robots will be used to do jobs that are hard, unsafe, and unpleasant. Human beings will then be free to do more creative and interesting jobs and to enjoy more free time. The money saved by using robots could be used to benefit everybody.

If things don't always work out this way, it won't be the robots' fault.

ROBOTS, ROBOTS EVERYWHERE

Have you ever met a real robot?

Many of the robots described in this book are in factories, nuclear power plants, or other places where most people never see them.

But robots are turning up in new places every day. Chances are good that you'll meet one of them sometime soon.

You may already have seen Silent Sam, the robot flagman who is used to direct traffic in many states. As robots go, Sam is not very smart. But he is very good at doing a dangerous job. Silent Sam was invented after a number of human flag-

47

A robot flagman
directing traffic.

48

men were killed in accidents while directing traffic on superhighways. Sam can stand in the middle of a busy highway with traffic whizzing past him on both sides. And because he is slightly larger than life, he is easier for motorists to see.

If you ever study to be a doctor or a nurse, your first patients may be robots. Sim One is a robot patient who is already in use training medical students at the University of Southern California. Sim has a heartbeat, a pulse, and a soft plas-

Sim One on the operating table.

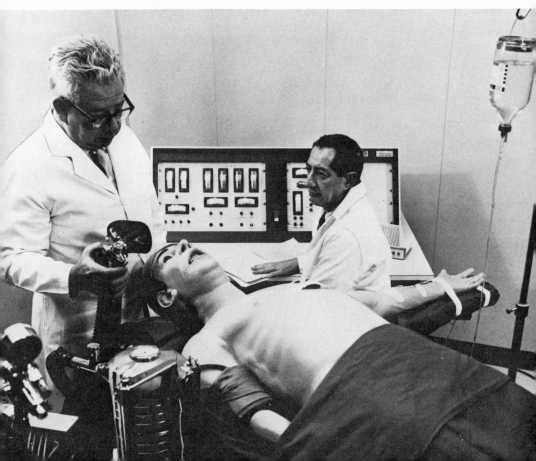

tic skin that looks very real. Students can practice giving Sim anesthesia. If they make a mistake, Sim will turn blue and go into cardiac arrest!

Hospitals are interested in other kinds of robots, too. The machines which are used to keep very ill people alive have become so complicated that some planners have thought about using robot nurses to keep an eye on them. Another possibility is that robots will be used to interview new patients. One hospital already tried using robot interviewers, and to everyone's surprise, patients gave more information to the robots than they did to humans doing the same job. Perhaps they were less embarrassed about giving personal information when no one but a robot was listening!

Another good place to look for robots is in a very large office building. About 250 of the country's biggest ones now use robot messenger carts to deliver papers and packages. The robot carts follow an invisible chemical trail sprayed along the hallways. They even ride the elevators and get off at the correct floor.

Until very recently, robots were definitely city creatures. But in the future, some robots may find work on farms. Australian sheep ranchers have

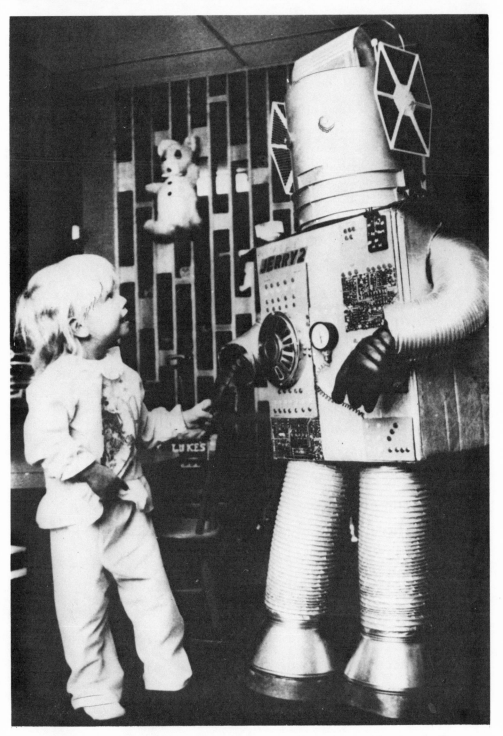

"Jerry 2," built by 8 year-old Jerry Miller and his older brother
Scott, visits a young hospital patient.

been testing a robot sheep shearer, and some poultry farmers in the United States have been thinking about using robots to pluck chickens and prepare them for market. It is possible that someday very large farms will have a whole staff of robot hired hands—including robot tractor drivers, robot fruit pickers, and robot shepherds.

There is almost no end to the number of jobs robots *might* be doing someday soon. It might be possible to build robot file clerks and robot bank tellers, robot police patrols and robot babysitters, robot translators and robot teachers. But this does not mean that robots would necessarily do these jobs better than human beings.

A human being can do many different things without even thinking. A robot has to have special instructions for every situation. For example, even the most up-to-date "seeing" robot does not know about shadows. Unless it has been told to do otherwise, a robot might spend all day trying to pick up a shadow. The same robot would have to have more instructions to deal with colors, and still more to deal with the fact that objects are not flat but three dimensional.

A robot cannot compare with a human being,

A life-sized robot named Goro makes friends during a visit to a Japanese kindergarten.

but robots *are* much smarter than other machines. Most machines are built to do a single job, but a robot can be reprogrammed and moved from one job to another. Where jobs are already done mostly by machine, a robot sometimes has an advantage. It can replace both the machine *and* its human operator.

For the time being, robots are most likely to be found doing jobs that are either very boring or very dangerous. But there is also a more interesting reason for using robots—because they are fun.

Toy robots far outnumber working robots in the world today. The Japanese, who are the biggest robot fans in the world, have designed life-size toy robots which sometimes make surprise appearances at children's playgrounds. Some major corporations—including the makers of Coca-Cola—have begun to use robot salesmen, just because the robots attract so much attention. Even the robot toys found in any department store can do things that would have seemed very advanced to scientists a few decades ago.

A ROBOT
IN THE HOUSE

The first question that most people ask when they hear about robots is "When will I be able to have a robot servant?"

A robot of one's very own—to do housework and errands—is the dream that has inspired many young scientists and inventors. Although the large companies that build working robots for industry are not very interested in designing robot servants, a number have been created by independent inventors and hobbyists working in their own homes.

Arok, the mechanical servant mentioned in

Arok walking the dog.

our robot quiz, is probably the most famous household robot in existence today. He is the invention of electrical engineer Ben Skora and was built out of about $200 worth of secondhand machinery and scrap—old refrigerator generators, auto parts, and even hoses from a discarded clothes dryer. Arok has an FM radio receiver in his brain and takes orders from Mr. Skora by remote control.

Mr. Skora admits that his robot servant has never actually saved him any work. Building Arok took many hours of labor, and even when Arok is operating perfectly, he has to be watched every minute. But the inventor feels that the fun of seeing his neighbors' faces when Arok takes out the garbage makes all his trouble worthwhile. The Skoras especially enjoy sending Arok into their local MacDonald's to pick up orders for them.

Other independent inventors have designed robots to do specialized jobs. An Englishman named Dennis Weston built a robot that could manage a number of household chores, including washing the family car. This robot, called Tinker, saved its owner muscle power but not time. Before Tinker could wash any given car it had to be programmed to "memorize" the car's shape. The programming took about four hours.

Tinker's counterpart in the United States is Mowbot. As you might guess from its name, this robot's specialty is mowing lawns.

Homemade robots give their owners lots of satisfaction, and they can do some useful jobs, such as vacuuming the rugs, answering the door, and serving cold drinks on a tray. But unfortunately, the day when you can tell a robot to clean the house while you go out to have a good time has not yet arrived.

Before a robot could be trained to work on its own, it would have to be able to make many decisions. It would have to know the difference between a bottle of furniture polish and a bottle of milk—and the difference between your pet cat and a dust mop.

Many experts believe that a practical robot servant could be designed, perhaps as soon as fifteen or twenty years from now. However, such a robot would cost a great deal of money—more than a whole houseful of labor-saving devices. What's more, many of the engineers and scientists

A robot servant would have to know the difference between
your pet cat and a dust mop.

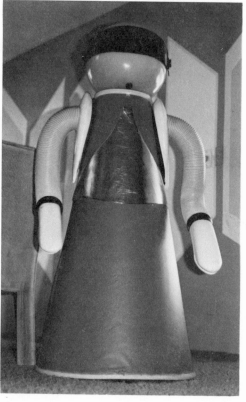

It's so nice to have a robot in the house . . . Klatu, a prototype of the Quasar household robot, in the kitchen of its owners, Tony and Eileen Reichelt.

who build robots for industry think that any machine smart enough to do housework would be too good for the job.

These experts may be right in thinking that robot servants are not a very practical idea, but this doesn't stop people from wanting them. One company, Quasar Industries, has already announced plans to sell robot servants to the public. Quasar's robots will be programmed to recognize the voices of members of their "families," and Quasar also claims that they will be able to tutor children, sound an alarm to scare away burglars, and even to keep watch over an infant or a bedridden adult. The company also promises to have a staff of human "robot doctors" who will make house calls if the robot breaks down.

This sounds wonderful, but remember, such a robot will cost thousands of dollars and it will still not be able to do many things that any child could learn to do in a few minutes.

For people who want a robot mainly for fun and companionship, a robot pet might be a better solution. Several years ago, a group called the United States Robotics Society suggested that it would be possible to build a robot pet that would

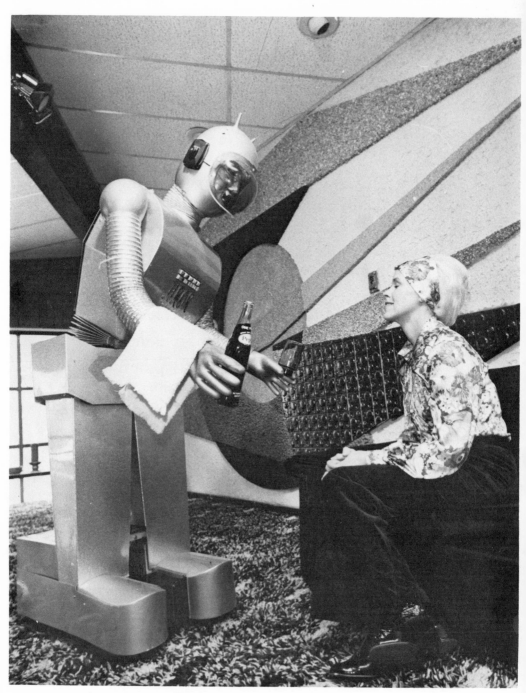

Arok entertains a visitor.

be warm and furry and have an appealing face. It could be programmed to purr when petted and to respond to the sound of its owner's voice. Naturally, it would not have to be fed or walked like a real animal.

If you would really like to have a robot around your house, either as a servant or as a pet, you will probably be able to do so someday. But don't be surprised if you spend more time taking care of your robot than it spends taking care of you.

The Hardiman exoskeleton.

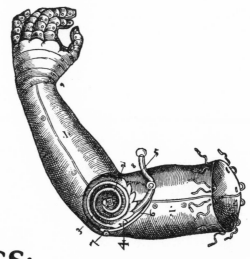

CYBORGS:
PART MAN—PART MACHINE

Many working robots do their jobs well, even though they do not look or act very human. But there are practical reasons for trying to build machines that can move, think, and even talk as humans do.

Engineers have long realized that their best creations often fall short of the wonderful designs that nature has built into living creatures. Today, many of them try to borrow ideas from biology and apply them to technology. This approach is called *bionics*—a word that is short for "biological electronics."

One original use of bionics is Hardiman, a robot skeleton built by the General Electric Company. The human being who straps himself inside Hardiman's big metal frame must feel like a superhero! Hardiman can lift up to 1,500 pounds, but to its human operator, the weight feels like only 60 pounds.

Working with Hardiman can be tricky, though. Hardiman magnifies human muscle power many times over. If the man or woman operating the robot skeleton moves too quickly or uses too much muscle power, Hardiman can swing out of control. Its mechanical muscles are so strong that they might break the arms and legs of a careless or unskilled operator.

Robot parts like the Hardiman skeleton can be used to make people stronger. But the advantages work both ways. Human control also makes robots less clumsy.

Robots that work with radioactive materials or delicate machinery can do a lot of damage if they are all thumbs. To give the robots better control, some are equipped with a "slave arm" that copies the movements of a human arm. A person sitting at the robot's control panel simply moves

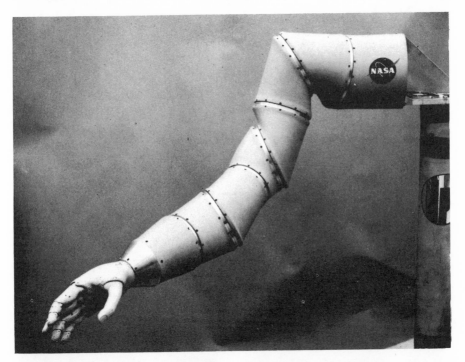

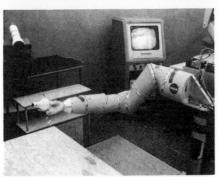 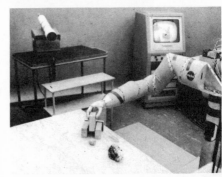

This robot slave arm was developed from a design for an astronaut's space suit.

his hand as if he were doing the work himself. The slave arm does the actual work by remote control—even though the robot may be many miles away from its operator, on the floor of the ocean or even in outer space.

The slave arm is just one example of an invention that was developed for robots, but which turned out to be useful in the field of medicine as well. Scientists are already using some of the devices from the slave arm to create better artificial arms for the handicapped. One such invention is a lifelike artificial hand that can be controlled by muscles in the wearer's arm. A still more complex hand, for people who have no arm muscles at all, responds when the wearer shrugs his shoulders or moves his chin in a certain way. Eventually, artificial arms might take orders directly from the brain, just as real arms do.

Another device we may see more of in the future is a metal skeleton—much lighter than Hardiman. Men and women who would otherwise be confined to a wheelchair would be able to walk upright when wearing this skeleton. They could then climb stairs, sit in ordinary chairs, and go many places where a wheelchair cannot operate.

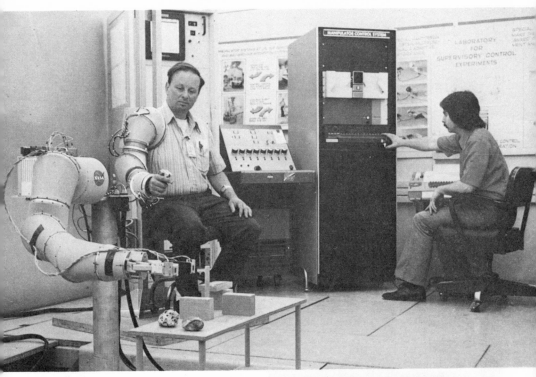

The slave arm and a human operator.

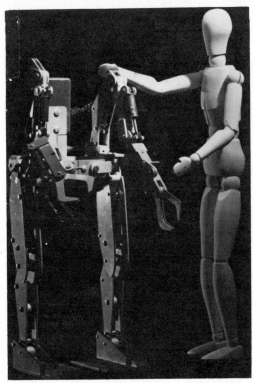

Another version of Hardiman.

Perhaps someday it will be possible to build a robot so lifelike that it could pass for human. But long before this happens, we will probably see much more of *cyborgs*—man-machine combinations. Many experts think that cyborgs will be the true robots of the future.

Cyborgs are well known today because of a writer named Martin Caidin whose ideas were used in two popular TV series—"The Six Million Dollar Man" and "The Six Million Dollar Woman." These series were about a man and a woman whose lives had been saved by bionics; as a result the hero and heroine were not just as good as new, but stronger and tougher than any normal human being. A few viewers didn't realize that these shows were fiction. The designers of artificial arms and legs sometimes receive letters asking for bionic parts like the ones shown in these television series.

Bionic parts that are better than flesh and blood do not exist. But their use as replacement parts when human bodies fail is becoming more common. And some scientists have even suggested that we might eventually use artificial parts to modify healthy people—so that they can live on other planets, or at the bottom of the ocean.

The idea of meeting cyborgs, or bionic men and women, in real life might seem creepy. But over 100,000 people already wear pacemaker machines to keep their hearts running properly. Many more have had broken bones repaired with pieces of plastic or metal. Technically, these people have become cyborgs.

It is hard to think of a good reason for building a completely lifelike robot. To do so would take millions of dollars and many years and, no

An inside look at an android, from the TV production "Westworld."

matter what we see in the movies or on TV, no mad scientist could possibly design such a robot in his basement laboratory.

On the other hand, the public is usually willing to spend large amounts of money if it leads to medical discoveries that enable people to live longer and healthier lives. For this reason, you can expect that during your lifetime you will see many important advances in the field of bionic medicine. The Bionic Man and Bionic Woman may be less farfetched than many of the robots we meet in the realm of science fiction.

Sim One.

ROBOTS IN OUTER SPACE

In science fiction, robots and space travel seem to go together. In real life, robots have already proven themselves to be the true pioneers of space exploration. Although no human being has yet landed on Mars, robots went there years ago.

In the summer of 1976, two American space vehicles landed on the surface of Mars. These Viking Landers looked like big metal crabs. They are considered robots, however, because each Lander vehicle did the work, not just of one astronaut, but of an entire team of scientific investigators.

NASA'S *Viking Lander at work on the surface of Mars, as envisioned by an earth-bound artist.*

Each of the Viking Landers had a long metal arm that could reach out and scoop up samples of Martian soil. The robot arm would then drop the soil samples into a special compartment that was actually a portable scientific laboratory. Experiments with the soil were done right there on the spot.

In addition to doing scientific tests, the Viking Landers took photographs of the surface of Mars. All of the Landers' movements were controlled by commands radioed from earth.

Robots will undertake many more dangerous space missions in the future.

For example, almost every movie ever made about space travel has a scene where the spaceship breaks down and a member of the crew has to go outside in a pressure suit to make repairs. This is always one of the most suspenseful moments in the movie. One false step and the crew member will be doomed to float through space forever.

Actually, such in-flight repairs will be made by robot mechanics. The first of these robots has been designed by NASA for use on the space shuttle mission. It will be able to take orders either from the crew members on board or from ground control.

The Space Horse mentioned in the robot quiz on page 12 is another kind of robot that may someday be used in space exploration. It is one of several robot designs that NASA has tested for helping astronauts move about on planets very different from our own.

Robots haven't always been welcome in the space program. In the beginning, many people who worked in the program felt that human beings deserved the chance to prove what they could do in outer space. Some people thought that using robots took the adventure out of space travel and, in the long run, robots would break down and ruin important missions years in the planning.

No one would deny that human astronauts can do many things that robots cannot. But today robots have become accepted partners in the space program. Robots have succeeded on a number of missions that would have been too dangerous and too expensive to accomplish with human beings.

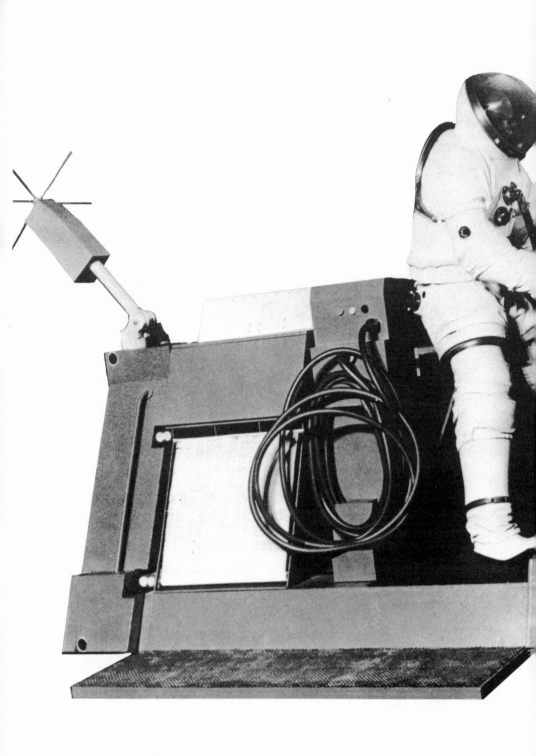

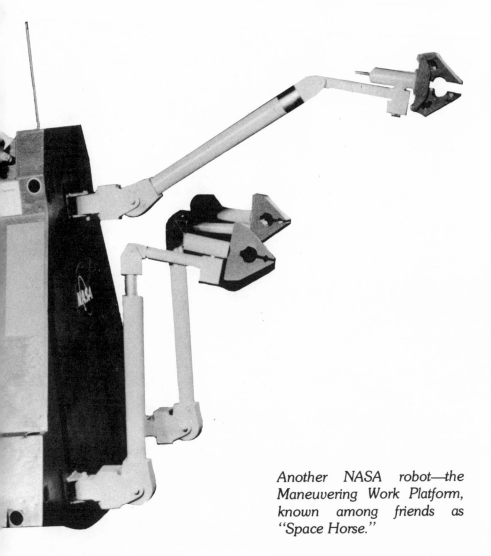

Another NASA robot—the Maneuvering Work Platform, known among friends as "Space Horse."

Overleaf: An artist's version of the Space Taxi, designed for flight repair work.

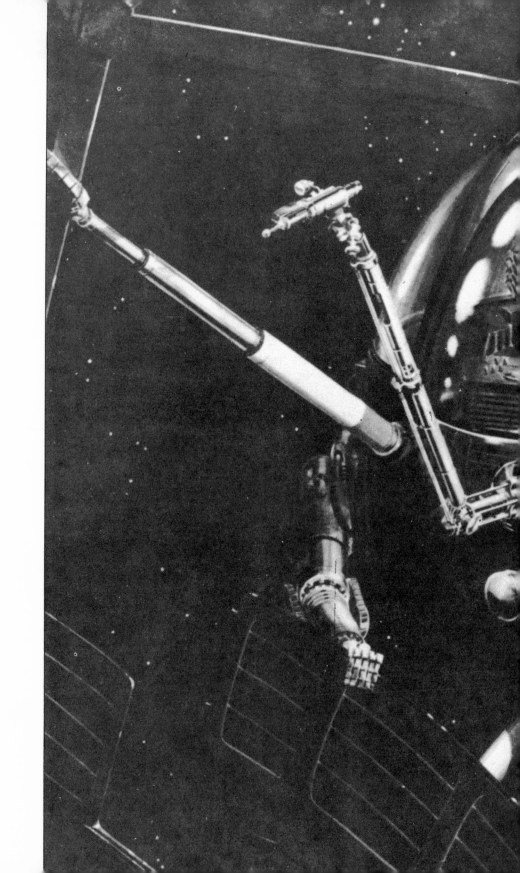

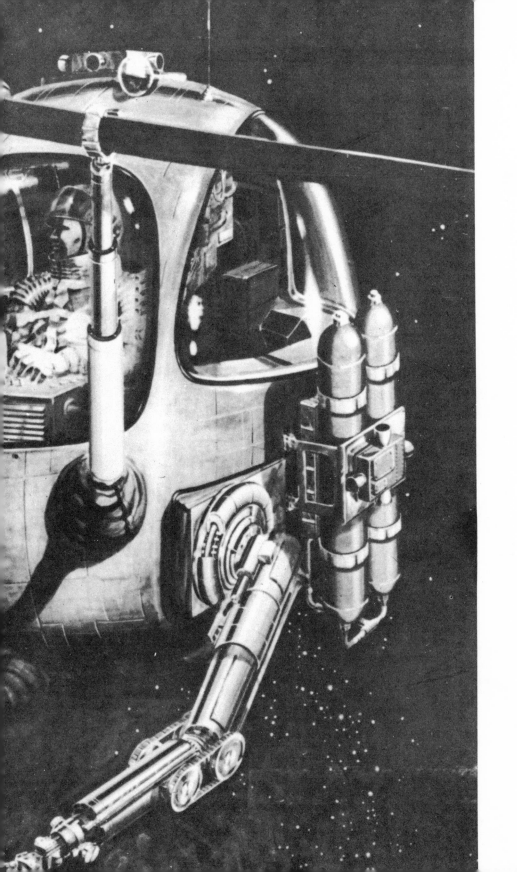

Leachim teaching fourth graders in the Bronx, New York.

TALKING ROBOTS

Of all the robots that exist today, robots that can talk are the most fun. One of the most interesting ones was named Leachim, and it worked for several years as a teacher's helper in a fourth grade class in the Bronx, New York. The class's regular teacher, Mrs. Gail Freeman, wished that she had a tutor to give individual help to her students. Fortunately, her husband, Dr. Michael Freeman, knew a lot about robots. He had built his own robot for fun when he was thirteen years old, and he decided that he could also build a robot tutor for his wife's class.

The result was Leachim. (Notice that Leachim is *almost* Michael spelled backwards.) Leachim was six feet tall and had plastic pipes for arms and flashing blue light bulbs for eyes. He had memorized an entire encyclopedia, the *Guinness Book of World Records,* and some fourth grade textbooks. He also knew all the children's names and how well they were doing in their schoolwork.

The students communicated with Leachim by dialing the answers to multiple-choice questions on a telephone dial attached to the robot's chest. But Leachim himself could talk. When one of his pupils gave a wrong answer, he would say "NOT CORRECT . . . NOT CORRECT" and give a make-up homework assignment. When someone came up with a right answer, Leachim would tell a joke or a riddle. He could even discuss sports.

When Leachim retired in 1975, the students in Mrs. Freeman's class were very disappointed. But programming Leachim so that he could keep up with his students had been a lot of work for Dr. Freeman.

Later, Dr. Freeman invented a much simpler and smaller robot called 2-XL which is used in schools and sold in toy stores. Like many of the robot toys sold today, it can do things that would have amazed people only ten or twenty years ago.

Another very impressive talking robot is Kurzie—short for the Kurzweil Reading Machine.

Kurzie does not look like an android robot. If anything, it looks like a cousin of a Xerox machine. But this doesn't matter to Kurzie's users, because they are blind. What does matter is that Kurzie will read books aloud to them.

To use the Kurzweil machine, a blind person places an open book face down on Kurzie's glass panel. Kurzie then reads those pages. Users listen to Kurzie through earphones, so that they will not disturb anyone working nearby.

Kurzie doesn't always pronounce every word perfectly. But no one can accuse it of not trying. In fact, one of the problems Kurzie's users have is that it will try to read anything set in front of it. If a book has pictures, Kurzie will try to "read" them too—but the result is a lot of nonsense syllables.

Blind people who use the Kurzweil Reading Machine soon learn how to correct these mistakes. They can even get Kurzie to spell out words they don't understand and to repeat parts of books they want to hear again. Kurzie is more patient than many human readers.

In between questions, the robot would make small talk and tell jokes.

ROBOT HOAXES

A talking robot can seem almost human. But don't be fooled.

No one has yet invented a robot that can carry on a sensible conversation. Robots *can* be programmed to ask questions and to answer them. But if a human being changes the subject, the robot is lost. Robots have no imagination.

A few years ago a group called ASMOF (The American Superior Mind Foundation) toured several big U.S. cities with a robot that was supposed to be a "genius." Audiences came to watch this robot perform. They asked the robot the hardest questions they could think of, and the robot almost always answered correctly. In between questions, the robot would make small talk and tell jokes.

Some reporters thought that this robot was just too good to be true. And they were right. It turned out that the robot was wired by radio to a command post several blocks away. Its answers were dictated by a human being, with the help of a shelf full of reference books and a panel of human experts.

Machines have changed a lot in the two hundred years since Baron von Kempelen's chess player amazed Europe. But human nature has not changed at all. Watch out for robot hoaxes.

ROBOTS: GOOD AND EVIL

Meeting a robot is usually fun. Almost no one is afraid of real robots, but robots in science fiction are another story. They often turn into monsters, destroying their creators and harming innocent people.

By 1939, there were so many books and short stories about evil robots that science fiction writer Isaac Asimov decided to speak up in the robots' defense.

Asimov felt that the robots of the future would probably be at least as trustworthy as human beings. To prove that good robots could be as interesting as evil ones, he wrote a series of stories about robots that were programmed to obey three basic laws.

THE LAWS OF ROBOTICS

1. A robot may not injure a human being, or through inaction allow a human being to come to harm.
2. A robot must obey the orders given it by human beings, except when such orders would conflict with the First Law.
3. A robot must protect its own existence as long as such protection does not conflict with the First and Second Laws.

Of course, these laws weren't foolproof. They often went wrong in unpredictable ways. That's what made Asimov's stories so interesting.

Many other writers agreed with Isaac Asimov that robot villains had become boring. Soon, imaginary robots of all kinds were obeying Asimov's laws. When a robot did turn evil—like the computer-robot HAL in the movie *2001*—there was usually some attempt to explain why Asimov's laws did not hold true.

For example, HAL's evil deeds were actually the fault of the scientists who had programmed him with contradictory orders. HAL was supposed to be perfect, and when he was faced with orders he could not possibly obey, he destroyed the crew of his spaceship so that his failure would never be discovered.

Asimov's laws are so well known that many people believe that they have been built into real-life robots. Unfortunately, this is not true.

Today, robots are being used as security guards and patrolmen. They may someday be used as weapons of war.

Armies and police forces became interested in robots because they could *save* lives by taking over some of the most dangerous jobs that soldiers and policemen have to do.

The RMIU—the Canadian Mountie robot described in the robot quiz on page 12—can search for hidden bombs and defuse them. It can also act as a go-between in negotiations with terrorists. A similar robot is used in Belfast, Northern Ireland, where terrorist bombings are common.

A robot fireman can move right into a burning building and put out the flames without fear of injury. It can also fight industrial fires, which can become too hot for human firemen.

"The Beetle," a 1960's robot designed to work with nuclear rockets.

A robot security guard can patrol a large area very quickly.

Robots will not actually carry weapons until their builders can figure out a way to make sure that the robots won't attack their own side—or innocent bystanders. But someday war robots could

The fear that machines will turn against us is almost as old as machines themselves. This cartoon was drawn in 1882.

be very destructive. Some military planners believe that the wars of the future will be fought in outer space by robots and remote-controlled weapons.

No one knows what such wars would be like. Perhaps the robots would do all the fighting, but people back on Earth would have to work very hard to build and pay for such expensive "soldiers." In the process, whole countries might become slaves to their robot armies. Or "space soldiers" might be equipped with terrible weapons, such as laser "cannons" which could destroy whole cities.

When Asimov wrote his laws he was thinking about the old fear that robots would turn against their creators—either accidentally or on purpose. Today, there is more danger that robot weapons will do their jobs too well.

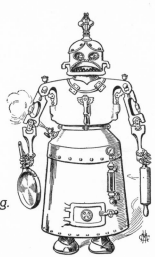

The cook of the future? A 1906 drawing.

ROBOTS OF TOMORROW

Will robots ever be smarter than people?

Will they ever have feelings and emotions, just as human beings do?

Will they take over all the jobs in the world, leaving the rest of us with nothing useful to do?

These questions are asked all the time by people who are interested in *robotics*—the science of robot design.

Most robotics experts who work with the day-to-day problems of building robots say that there is nothing to worry about. No matter how "smart" a robot gets, it will always be just a machine.

Artists of the 1920's and 1930's imagined robots that looked like pot-bellied stoves or mechanical octopuses.

This is certainly true of today's robots. They can learn. They have memories. But they cannot think creatively the way a person does.

However, some philosophers have already begun to argue about whether or not it is possible for a robot to have emotions. Although the idea of a machine feeling happy or sad may seem to go against common sense, it's not so easy to prove that this could not happen. For one thing, we don't really know what emotions are; all we know is that we have them. If a machine said that it had feelings too, how could we be sure that it was wrong?

Some scientists have suggested that the robots of the future will not even have electronic brains of the kind that are built today. Instead, they might have jellylike brains made of blobs of protein.

Another interesting possibility was raised as long ago as the 1940's by a mathematician named John von Neumann. Von Neumann proposed that someday machines might be able to duplicate themselves.

Another scientist, Dr. Freeman Dyson, once suggested that these "von Neumann" machines could be used to colonize outer space. As soon as they landed on the surface of a distant planet, they would set to work building other machines which would then begin to change the planet's environment to make it more like Earth. Eventually, the colony of machines would be ready to welcome human settlers.

Predicting the future is a kind of a game. It is easy to think of kinds of robots that might be invented someday. But just because something might be done, that does not mean that it *will* be done.

As people become more concerned about the energy crisis, it's possible that we will decide we need fewer machines, not more machines. The robot might even become extinct, like the dinosaur.

On the other hand, new discoveries may make it possible to build robots that make conversation, cook gourmet meals, play football, write poetry, manage factories, judge court cases—and even design and build other robots more complicated than themselves.

One hundred years ago, no one would have imagined that someday robots would read to the

Someday robots may even play football.

This is a drawing of a "pedipulator"—an idea proposed some years ago for a Hardiman-type robot.

blind . . . put out fires . . . teach children . . . or perform scientific experiments on Mars. The robots of one hundred years from now may be just as hard for us to imagine.

GLOSSARY:
WHAT IS A ROBOT?

"I can't define a robot; but I know one when I see one."—Joseph Engleberger, President of Unimation, Inc., a robot manufacturing company.

Most people think that they know a robot when they see one. But when it comes to defining the word robot, even the experts cannot agree.

A **robot** is usually defined as a machine that looks *or* performs like a living creature. This is a good definition for everyday use, but most scientists feel that looks should not count. As far as they're concerned, only machines that can follow a set of complex instructions and do something to change their environment are real robots.

An **automaton** is any machine that works "on its own." A cuckoo clock is an example of an automaton because the cuckoo appears on the hour; no one has to push a button to make the cuckoo jump out of the clock. Some people use the word automaton to apply to robots, too.

An **android** is any machine that looks or acts human. The word android was used many years ago to describe some mechanical toys, or automatons. But today, it usually means a robot with soft, lifelike skin. Such robots are more likely to show up on TV or in the movies than in real life, but SIM ONE, the artificial hospital patient, is an example of a real android.

A **cyborg** is part robot and part human. The bionic man and woman in the shows *"The Six Million Dollar Man"* and *"The Six Million Dollar Woman"* are cyborgs.

ROBOT RECORDS

1. ***The World's Largest Robot*** was built for the Japanese world's fair Expo '70 in Osaka. This robot was twenty-four feet tall, and its body could be raised and lowered like an elevator. At the end of one of its arms was a platform big enough to hold several people.

2. ***The World's Most Expensive Robots*** were the Viking Landers built for the Viking Mars expeditions of 1976. These robots were also the most complex ever built. The whole project cost close to a billion dollars.

3. **The World's First Automatons** were mechanical birds built by the Chinese as early as 500 B.C. The first automatons that we know much about, however, were created by Hero of Alexandria, a Greek who lived in Egypt during the first century A.D. Hero's creations worked by water power.

4. **The First Walking Automaton.** George Moore's Walking Locomotive, built in 1893, was a life-sized automaton that looked like a medieval knight dressed in a suit of armor. It was steam-powered and could walk in circles at a speed of nine miles an hour.

5. **The First Talking Automaton.** In 1778, Baron von Kempelen, the same man who fooled people with the chess-playing Turk, demonstrated a talking automaton which was able to say such words as *opera, astronomy,* and *Constantinople.* A similar automaton, named Euphonia and designed by a German inventor named Joseph Faber, appeared in London in 1830. Euphonia worked by means of bellows which were attached to a keyboard operated by Faber. Many people suspected

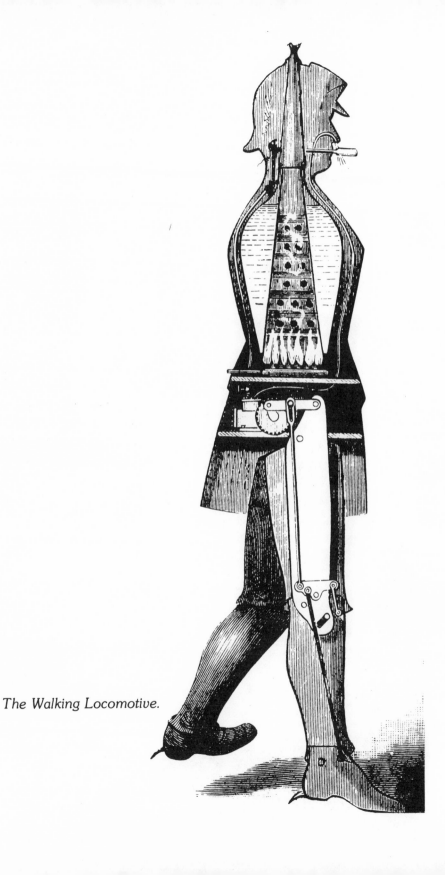

The Walking Locomotive.

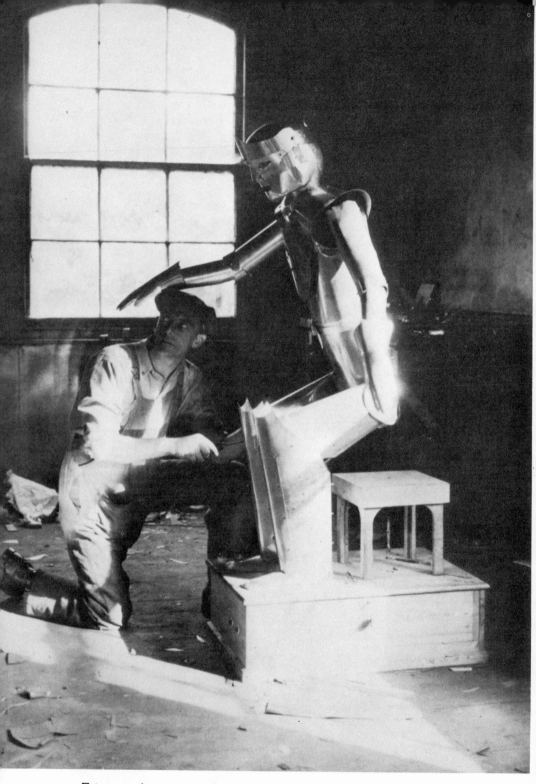

Eric, an aluminum robot inspired by the play RUR, was exhibited in England in 1927.

both of these automatons of being hoaxes, but no one was able to prove this.

6. ***The First Real Robot*** was probably Eric, designed and built in England in 1927 by a man who had seen Karel Čapek's play, *R.U.R.*

7. ***The Smallest Working Robot*** is a model of the industrial robot known as PUMA. It weighs only fifteen pounds.

8. There have been many ***Young Robot Builders.*** Dr. Meredith Thring, a British robot expert is said to have built his first robot when he was eleven years old. Jonathan Kaplan of New York City built his first robot when he was twelve and designed a new robot every year until he was eighteen.

9. ***Robots Who Attack Their Masters*** are more common in fiction than in real life. However, there is one documented case of an inventor who was killed when his robot's arm fell on him. Of course, this was an accident.

10. ***A Robot Chess Champion.*** In 1968, Scottish chess champion David Levy offered a prize of 500 English pounds (about $1,250) for any computer that could beat him at

chess. The prize was finally claimed in 1978 when Levy was defeated in a match against a computer-controlled robot arm. The match was held in Hamburg, Germany, but the robot's computer brain was located in Minneapolis, Minnesota!

11. **The Heaviest Robot Smoker.** Many of the demonstration robots of the 1930's smoked cigarettes or cigars, but the heaviest smoker of all was Elektro, whose pictures usually show him enveloped in a haze of smoke. In those days, the dangers of smoking were not well known; today, smoking robots are a rarity.

12. **A Robot Auto Mechanic,** designed at the Stanford Artificial Intelligence Laboratory, Stanford University, is capable of putting together a complete automobile water pump from a variety of parts spread out on a table. This robot may be the forerunner of robots which are capable of functioning in workshops, garages, and even in homes.

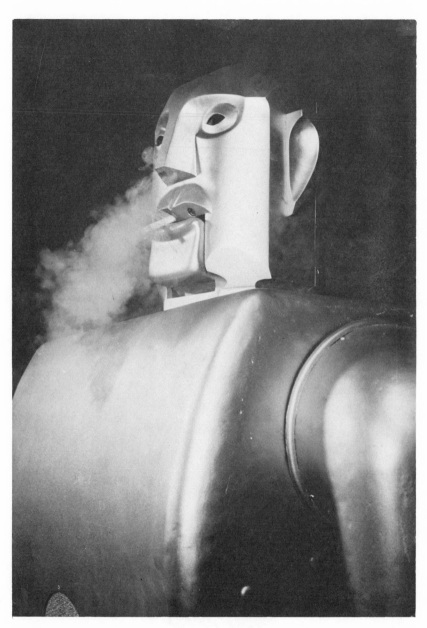

Electro.

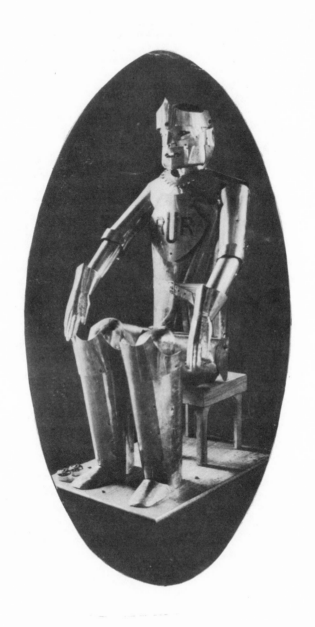

Picture Credits

The Bettmann Archives, Inc., 28

Cincinnati Milacron, 43

Crown Copyright, Victoria and Albert Museum, London, 16-17

Dr. Michael J. Freeman, 82

General Electric Corporation, 38, 39, 64, 69 bottom

Hughes Aircraft Company, 36

Copyright 1978 IEEE. Reprinted, with permission, from *IEEE Spectrum,* 31 (February 1978, page 12); 33, 34 (November 1978, page 63)

Illustrated London News, New York Public Library Picture Collection, 2, 106

Jet Propulsion Laboratory, California Institute of Technology, 69 top

Karakui Zui or *Illustrated Book of Mechanisms,* (Japan 1796), 18 top

Courtesy of Lucasfilm, Ltd. © Lucasfilm, Ltd. (LFL) 1977. All rights reserved, 10

From the MGM TV series "Beyond Westworld." © 1980, Metro-Goldwyn-Mayer, 71

Musée d'Art et d'Histoire, Neuchâtel, New York Public Library Picture Collection, 21

Museum of Modern Art, New York, 27

NASA, 67, 74-75, 78-79, 80-81

New York Public Library Picture Collection, 15, 16-17, 18 bottom, 19, 23, 89, 93, 95, 96, 105

New York Public Library, Rare Book Division, (from J. F. Racknitz, *Uber den Schachspieler*, [Leipzig, 1789]), 24

Prab Conveyors, Incorporated, 40

Radio Times Hulton Picture Library, 106

Quasar Industries, Inc., 55, 60 bottom

Queens Devices, Incorporated, 48

Unimation, Incorporated, 42

University of Southern California, School of Medicine, 49, 72

Westinghouse, 29, 109

Wide World Photos, 51, 53, 56, 60 top, 62, 92, 100

Selected Bibliography

Books:

Asimov, Isaac. *I, Robot.* Greenwich, Connecticut: Fawcett Crest Books, 1970.

——. *The Rest of the Robots.* Garden City, NY: Doubleday, 1964.

Boehn, Max von. *Puppets and Automata.* Translated by Joseph E. Nicoll. New York, NY: Dover Publications, 1972.

Cooke, Robert. *Improving on Nature, The Brave New World of Genetic Engineering.* New York, NY: Quadrangle/New York Times, 1977.

Geduld, Harry M. and Ronald Gottesman. *Robots Robots Robots.* Boston: New York Graphic Society (Little, Brown and Co.), 1978.

Heims, Stephen J. *John von Neumann and Herbert Wiener: From Mathematics to the Technologies of Life and Death.* Cambridge, Massachusetts: MIT Press, 1980.

Malone, Robert. *The Robot Book.* New York, NY: Harvest/HBJ, 1978.

Reichardt, Jasia. *Robots: Fact, Fiction and Prediction.* New York, NY: The Viking Press, 1978.

Safford, Edward L., Jr. *The Complete Handbook of Robotics.* Summit, Pennsylvania: Tab Books, 1978. A how-to-build-it guide for the *advanced* hobbyist.

Sagan, Carl. *Broca's Brain: Reflections on the Romance of Science.* New York, NY: Random House, 1979.

Articles:

Allan, Roger. "Three Amazing Micromice: Hitherto Undisclosed Details." *IEEE Spectrum,* November 1978.

Bylinsky, Gene. "The New Robots." *Fortune,* December 17, 1979.

Colligan, Douglas. "The Robots Are Coming." *New York,* July 30, 1979.

Denson, J. S., M.D. & Stephen Abrahamson, Ph.D. "A Computer-Controlled Patient Simulator." *The Journal of the American Medical Association,* April 21, 1969.

Morris, Donald. "In Illinois: A Better Robot." *Time,* August 14, 1979.

Reed, Fred. "The Robots Are Coming; The Robots Are Coming." *Next,* May/June 1980.

Schefter, Jim. "New Workers On The Assembly Line: Robots That Think." *Popular Science,* June 1980.

114

Index

Alpha (robot), 26, 28, 30, 43
Amazing Micro Mouse, 34, 35
Androids, 20-22, 102
   definition of, 20
Arok (robot servant), 12, 55, 57
American Superior Mind Foundation (ASMOF), 87, 88
Asimov, Isaac, 14, 89-91
Automaton, 20, 22, 24, 25
   definition of, 20, 24, 102
   chess player, 22-24
   world's first, 104
   first walking, 104
   first talking, 104

Bierce, Ambrose, 13
Biological electronics, 65, 66
Bionics, 65, 66, 70-72
Blue collar robots, 41-43

C3PO (robot), 11
Caidin, Martin, 70
Čapek, Karel, 14, 25, 107
Catty Wampus (robot), 34, 35
Computer controlled brain, 43
Computers, 35, 43
Cyborgs, 65-71, 102

Dyson, Dr. Freeman, 97

Electronic brains, 32, 35
Electro (robot), 12, 28, 30, 43, 107
Elmer (robot), 32, 33
Elsie (robot), 32, 33
Eric (robot), 107
Euphonia (automaton), 104, 105
Evil robots, 26, 89-91

Faber, Joseph, 104
Forbidden Planet, 14
Frankenstein, 22
Freeman, Mrs. Gail, 83, 84
Freeman, Michael, 83, 84

General Electric Co., 66
Guinness Book of World Records, 84

HAL (robot), 90, 91
Hardiman (robot), 66, 68
Hero of Alexandria, 104

Isabella, Queen, 20

Jacquet-Droz, 21, 22

Kaplan, Jonathan, 107
Kempelen, Baron von, 22, 88, 104
Kurzie (robot), 85
Kurzweill Reading Machine, 85

Lang, Fritz, 25, 26
Laser "cannons", 94
Laws of Robotics, 90
Leachim, (robot), 83, 84
Levy, David, 107, 108
London Radio Exposition (1932), 26
Luna, Don Alvaro, 17, 19

Mechanical body, 35
"Mechanical man", 15
Mechanical Men, Inc., 30
Mechanical toys, 15-17, 20
  dolls, 15
  lion, 16
  power for, 20
"Mechanical Turk", 22-24
Metal Skeleton, 68
Metropolis, 26
Micro Mouse, Amazing, 34-35
Midnight Flash (robot), 35
Mobot (robot), 37, 38, 39
Moore, George, 104
Moxon's Robot, 12, 14

NASA, 76, 77
Neumann, John von, 97
New York World's Fair (1939), 28

Pacemaker machine, 71
Poe, Edgar Allan, 22-24
PUMA (robot), 107

Quasar Industries, 61

R2-D2 (robot), 11
Remote control, 39, 40, 43, 57
RMIU (Robot Mobile Investigation Unit), 12, 91
Robbie (robot), 12, 14
Robot mechanics, 76, 77
Robots:
  auto mechanics, 108

baby sitters, 12
bomb defusers, 91
chess players, 12, 14, 107
compared to machines, 54
cost of, 57, 61, 103, 104
definition of, 31, 32, 101, 102
dogs, 12
"eyes" of, 37, 39, 43, 44, 52
evil, 26, 89, 91
on farms, 50, 52
as firemen, 91, 92
first, 11
first made for sale, 30
first working, 39, 107
future of, 95, 97
hoaxes, 87, 88
in hospitals, 50
imaginary, 11, 12, 14, 26
in industry, 41, 42, 46
largest, 103
limitations of, 32, 35, 52, 57, 58, 61, 66, 71, 87, 92, 95, 97
in medicine, 50, 68
mice, 33-35
mistakes by, 44, 90, 91
mobile, 37
name origin, 25
in offices, 50
as pets, 61, 63
reading by, 85
remote control of, 39, 40, 43, 47, 57, 68
security guards, 91
servants, 12, 55, 57, 58, 61, 63
skeletons, 66, 68
smallest, 107
smoking, 26, 108

talking, 12, 26, 83, 85
teaching, 12, 83-85
turtle, 32, 33
typist, 12, 14
RUR (Rossum's Universal Robots), 14, 25, 107

Shannon, Claude, 33, 35
Shelley, Mary, 22
Silent Sam (robot), 47, 49
Sim One (robot), 49, 50
"Six Million Dollar Man, The", 70, 102
"Six Million Dollar Woman, The", 70, 102
Skora Ben, 57
"slave arm," 57
Space Horse, The (robot), 12, 77
Sparko (robot), 12, 28, 30
Spectrum, 34
Stanford Artificial Intelligence Laboratory, 108
Star Wars, 11
Sulla (robot), 12, 13

Thring, Meredith, 107
Tinker (robot), 57, 58
toy robot, 54
2001: A Space Odyssey (movie), 90, 91

United States Robotic Society, 61, 63
Universal Mobile Robot (UNIMO), 37-39

University of Southern California, 49

Viking Lander (robot), 73, 76, 103, 104

Walter, William Grey, 32
Weston, Dennis, 57
World's Largest Robot, 103
World's Most Expensive Robot, 101, 103